YOU
ARE
UNSTOPPABLE

Reach Your Goals In Spite of Obstacles

RITA SIAW

YOU ARE UNSTOPPABLE

ISBN: 978-9988-2-8673-6

Direct all correspondence and inquiries to:

Rita Siaw
Associate Director, Adanu
Founder, Feminine Star Africa
P. O. Box 815,
Ho.
Email: ritlove_21@yahoo.com, rita@adanu.org

Other Book by Rita Siaw:
Cohesive Change for Future leaders.

Edited by:
TERRY MANTE
(TERRY MANTE EXCHANGE)

Design and layout by:
BOAFO BENJAMIN (0206027437)
TERRY MANTE EXCHANGE

ENDORSEMENTS

"This story of a tenacious, young woman who refused to settle for "No" as an answer will be a source of inspiration to many young people. Rita Siaw brings that same tenacity to her work in promoting education in her community. If she has done it, anyone can!"

Ruby Yayra Goka,
Mandela Washington Fellow,
Dentist/Author (GHANA)

"This book outlines a journey of perseverance, tenacity and determination. It serves as a light of hope in the darkest times. *You Are Unstoppable* is a guide for the youth, a direction toward success and a must read for those who want to live a purposeful life."

Dr. Annick Raissa Sidibe,
Mandela Washington Fellow,
Immunization Advocacy Initiative Project Officer,
WACSI (BURKINA FASO)

"It should be noted that for there to be any outstanding piece of literature such as this book; its author must be intimately connected to the subject. Rita Siaw is not only connected, but she 'lives' in her work. In so doing touching the lives of thousands of young girls from the rainforest, Ghana's Volta Region, where her Buem People are located. As a Nana of Buem Traditional Area, I have observed her work first-hand and provided some funding and technical support along the way. Thus I can validate my statement for eight years of association."

Dr. John David Arnold, aka Nana Bloti Omaboyo I,
Founder/CEO, PPEP Inc. (www.ppep.org)
(Arizona, USA)

"The advisory nature of Rita's book suggests that life's roadmap has so many winding curves. Read this book and learn from one of the best."

Gifty Mensah
Mandela Washington Fellow,
International Consultant-
Angie Brooks International Centre (ABIC) for Women's
Empowerment, Leadership Development, International Peace and
Security (GHANA)

iv

"Rita Siaw is an amazing fabulous woman, hands down! I am excited that she shares a bit more of her story in this book. The pieces of advice she gives in this book are priceless. Please take them seriously, don't wait to go round in circles before you come to the realization that there is actually a way out of your hassle."

Ama Duncan,
Mandela Washington Fellow
Founder, The Fabulous Woman Network
(GHANA)

"Rita Siaw is a gallant young woman who put the development of other people first. She is the epitome of a true role model and I recommend her book *You Are Unstoppable* to everyone to read and get helpful insights to excel in all endeavors."

Cecilia Fiaka,
Founder, Nneka Youth Foundation
(GHANA)

"This is an excellent masterpiece on self-development and potential-discovery coming from the stable of a great lady making waves across the personal development arena. Tap into its rich wisdom; leverage on its methods and capitalize on its rich repertoire of simple but deep principles to live by to lift you higher."

Conrad Kakraba,
Author, Lecturer and Former Ghana Television Newscaster
(GHANA)

"Rita Siaw is an amazing personality with a beautiful soul. She is a visionary who sees life the way it ought to be. Reading her story confirms that everyone can be what they set their minds to be and the only person who can stop you, is YOU."

Ketura Adams,
Mandela Washington Fellow
Founder, Kabash Love Foundation
(NIGERIA)

DEDICATION

This book is wholeheartedly dedicated to the hardworking women of Africa and other parts of the world.

ACKNOWLEDGEMENTS

I thank God for the ability to write this book.

Sincere appreciation goes to my parents who sacrificed their happiness to give us education.

Thanks to Bertrand Casaubon, who has been very instrumental in my life.

I am also grateful to Mr. Jos Acquah, former General Manager of Heritage FM for granting me a platform to unearth my potential.

I also thank all the individuals who shared their experiences to motivate the youth. I am especially grateful to Jean Francois Favory and Noella Wiyaala Nwadei in this regard.

To all the teachers and students of Likpe Nkwanta M/A Basic School, the Board and staff of Adanu, I appreciate your encouragement towards the completion of this book.

To my beloved husband Asko Tapio Nittyvuopio, thank you for complementing my life.

One of the secrets to success is to refuse to let temporary setbacks defeat us.

Mary Kay

CONTENTS

CHAPTER ONE

ERASE CHILDISH THOUGHTS

Childishness can be misleading

It was a sunny afternoon when I arrived at the premises of my former school almost seven months after graduating. The worn-out structures stood still as usual without any touch of beauty.

The administration was a place I hated while I was a student there. This was because, it was as a "law court" where student crimes were handled. Any one seen there was assumed to have "a serious case." I started praying in my mind not to meet that dreadful man *Okokobioko*. Okokobioko was a nickname our predecessors had given to our assistant headmaster. He was the house father for the boys' hostel and the head of Visual Arts Department. He also taught sculpture at various levels in the school.

All students feared him because he never had mercy on any one who got into trouble with him. I remembered he once grabbed me by the neck of my dress dragging me along just because I kept an "Afro". Afro was kept by many seniors, especially the girls because they wanted to perm their hair just after the last paper of the final examination.

The administration had a short wall with large windows that made it possible for whoever was in there to see you 100 metres away. I had returned to the school to check on the outcome of the final examinations. I mustered courage, walked into the room, greeted everyone and proceeded to the headmaster's office. After greeting him, he asked of my name and started rustling through a pile of pink sheets. "God help me pass with good grades", I prayed in my mind as if some magic could change my result instantly. Within fifteen minutes, he handed over a pink-colored sheet of paper to me. I took it, thanked, him and walked out without looking back.

After a few minutes of walking, I flipped the paper to check my grades. I had the shock of my life; "Five passes? Oh my God! Why me? This can't take me anywhere", I exclaimed. "What am I going to do with this?" I asked; as if someone else wrote the examinations for me. I went home worried and could not show the result boldly to my dad as I used to do those days when I had passed my end of term examinations.

I lay on my bed condemning myself for failing three courses. There was nowhere I could conjure a different result slip to enable me get into any tertiary institution. I finally came to terms with the fact that it was too late and there was nothing I could do about it. For weeks, I was so disturbed not knowing what to do. What I did to comfort

2

myself was shamelessly blaming poverty for being the root of all my catastrophes. I could not face the fact that I was also a contributing factor to my failure.

Whenever the word "future" was mentioned, it seemed so far away. I used to think I was too young to be in charge of my life. Little did I know that time flew by very fast and often went unnoticed. I did waste some time during my senior high school education; time I could have put into my private studies, time I could have leveraged to ask for support and time I could have spent doing group work with other classmates.

There are certain things that can really throw you off board in your quest for success. One of them is to having a childish mindset. This simply means thinking like a child, although you are no longer a child. This is when a young adult still thinks and behaves like a child. This is when one refuses to grow out of his or her average thinking and is unable to differentiate between what is necessary and what is not.

Childishness blinds us most of the time, and we end up not seeing the enormous opportunities available, so they pass us by without utilizing them. Let's take a look at some questions that can help you know if you are missing out on opportunities. I want you to look deep inside your heart and be very sincere to yourself in answering them. How many opportunities passed you by due to your own negligence? What would you have achieved if you had grabbed those opportunities?

In my childishness, I thought my parents, teachers and any elderly person who advised me said almost the same things; "Learn hard, stop playing, concentrate on your books and make us proud." I felt it was a bother at that time and was just too much to take in. These words were whining in my ears so much that, as soon as an elderly person called me, I knew what the person was going to say. Sometimes, as they began a sentence, I ended it in my mind even before they completed the statement. I never knew the essence of their words until I received my result slip.

As a young person, your parents are responsible for your well-being but not for your actions. Don't forget that your actions and inactions determine what you can become. Therefore, you cannot blame others for the outcome of your actions and inactions.

Facing life as a young person

The relevance of the facts I am sharing with you is to save you from making the same mistakes I made. I took the wrong turn to learn but I want you to learn from my experience. I was given several pieces of advice which I did not take very seriously until failure embraced me with shame. You are still in school. You can do something and make a difference now!

Don't get irritated with the advice of parents, guardians and teachers. Count yourself lucky to have them give you these insights into life. Some people never got it that way; some have lost their parents and live with relatives or people who don't care about their welfare.

So, if you have parents who love and care a lot about you, you must really appreciate them. I would not like you to live to regret one day as I did the day I received my results. Due to my failure, it took me a long time to show it to my dad. Worst of all, it took me two years to make up for the losses; years I could have used profitably to pursue my dreams. That was the price I had to pay for playing lazy as a student. My failure reminded me a lot about how much time I had wasted.

All hope is not lost when you fail at a point in time; there is still room for improvement if only you can wake up from your slumber.

One morning I sat down contemplating on what to do next. I decided that it would be good to learn a trade from my aunty since she was a seamstress. I chose this option because I didn't want to stay home doing nothing. I wanted to have a job and earn money to improve my life. I discussed it with my dad who hated the idea, as he has always wanted me to be a topmost public servant heading a government branch. He didn't waste time in sending me back to my aunty one sunny afternoon to look for a remedial school and begin preparations to re-write the exam.

A few days after my arrival, my aunty asked about my results. "What should I tell her?" My inner voice exclaimed. I decided to just keep quiet over my results because of the shame of letting the rotten cat out of the bag. I gathered the courage knowing very well how persistent she can be. When I told her I had five passes with aggregate 22, I was surprised at her reaction, "You did very well", she exclaimed. Others could not even get two papers, and you have five. You are good and can do better if you re-sit". Instantly, I knew my dad put those words in her mouth. I could remember my dad saying almost the same phrase. She cited an example of her friend's daughter who had just one paper out of eight. Listening to these words, I got soaked with a strong desire to go back to join the remedial class and rewrite my papers.

Now to you reading this, remember that we all encounter difficulties but our tenacity and perseverance keep us going. It is how we handle ourselves in challenges that make us winners or losers. In fact, that was a defining moment for me, a moment where someone saw something good in my failure; even when I had given up on myself. My aunt's words were exactly what I needed at that moment. ˙Anyone in such a situation would need reassurance that things could turn around for their good if they work at it.

So even if no one says them to you, you've got to say them to yourself. I brushed off the idea of learning a trade since that wasn't really my dream. I contacted a few friends to inquire about remedial classes in the city. They told me all I needed to know. In less than a month, I got myself registered to re-sit for the exams. I then started chasing after remedial classes that were available. I finally chose the cheapest to be able to pay the bills.

At the time, there was not enough money to cater for the tuition fees, so I decided to look for a job to support myself. I got a pupil teaching job which gave me ample time to go for tuition and study after school. I continued like that for months; doing pupil teaching and at the same time attending remedial classes. One thing about life is, when you think things are getting better and you begin to breathe a sigh of relief, then an unexpected situation hits you.

Don't breathe a sigh of relief until you are off the hook holding you down.

It was a Tuesday morning when my aunty sat me down and said she was getting married in two months. The good news that my aunty was getting married in few months brought lots of worries. I began to think of where to I would live when she eventually moved in with her husband since we were living in a rented single room. I was so confused and wondered if my dreams were going to be shattered forever. Someone's joy was slowly paddling me into pain. I was down again with so much thinking, wondering how to raise money to rent a place of my own. In the face of this pain, I learnt that I don't always have to look to others for help. I had to start taking responsibility for myself. I professed to myself that so long as I had life, I would do my very best to stay focused on my dreams.

Challenges cause you to use your creativity to sort yourself out. I had to start looking for accommodation as the time was fast-approaching. She finally broke the news of moving out to join her husband in two weeks. This was telling me indirectly to find a way of accommodating myself. I thought it was impossible getting accommodation because I was very young and very tiny as well. I thought no one would take me seriously if I asked to rent their room. I kept wondering which landlord will rent a room to a little girl like me. I knew they would ask me to bring my parents. I could not even reach any of them since they didn't have a phone. Quickly, I thought of falling on a friend who would pose as though he was renting the place and say he was my uncle.

I guess you are wondering whether my parents cared at all. Yes! They did and still do. I personally decided to face all these simply because my parents went back to the village after losing their business in the city. They decided to start working as peasant farmers instead. I knew very well that they were doing their very best to cater for the numerous children they had. For that matter, I saw their hard work and struggles and wanted to do the little I could to support them in taking care of my siblings.

I knew my parents loved us so much and would do anything for us if they had the means to. They helped me through high school and I found it very difficult going back to sit and look at their faces for survival. I chose to help myself to further my education and be able to support my siblings. I knew I had to start taking responsibility for myself in order to live my dreams and not to live with regret in my old age. This is because my parents' situation and hardship was a life I never wanted.

I finally managed to secure a single room and began life all alone. My independence was short lived as two of my younger siblings had to come and live with me to attend a good school. I was just a teenager then. Initially, I found it extremely difficult parenting two young girls who wanted their own ways and were very stubborn sometimes. My greatest concern was that I was also an adolescent who needed to be guided. Yet, I ended up taking care of other adolescents. How was I to coach these two girls to become responsible women while I was only a child too?

The challenges we face and overcome determine our strength and show the true person we are inside.

Despite all those worries, I took them as my own kids, I advised them when I had to and provided their needs. I became their house teacher, a mentor and a mother. Life went on this way until one completed junior high school with very good grades to my amazement.

I am sharing all these experiences to draw your attention to the fact that life is not a straight path, and that, unforeseen events will always occur. As a young person, you should always be prepared to adapt to such conditions. Find positive means to make things work out to your advantage. Manage the problem you are facing so that it doesn't go beyond your control. Having total control over those situations is what is necessary. Remember, looking for ways and means to evade challenges today would only bring them back to you in a grim way later on.

As a young person, I would also urge you to gradually assist your family as you begin to get settled. Don't start focusing on your independence forgetting that you must look out for your younger siblings. You need to help them with the knowledge you have acquired and the little resource you have in other to secure their self-reliance.

10

Without this, you will carry their burdens when they are aged and are jobless. *"Fishing for a man serves him for a moment, but teaching him how to fish serves him a lifetime!"* This saying has always kept me going day by day; it is why I gathered courage to support my siblings. I am rest assured that with this, I will have a stress-free life in the near future.

It's better to stretch your hand to help a brother climb a ladder together than to get up there and throw the cramps of what you eat to him.

To pave a way through the hassle, you have to stay away from childishness and work in unison with other players for a better life.

CHAPTER TWO

CHALLENGES FACING THE YOUTH

Struggle with pride

One of the major problems with youthfulness is pride. We tend to feel we know more than our parents who gave birth to us. This struggle comes with adolescence where we begin to develop emotionally and physically; this makes us feel equal to adults. We seem to forget that we are still undergoing transformation in a child's body. Sometimes, this leads to disobedience and disregard for rules and directives. This is the starting point of all the other challenges I will be outlining as we progress in this chapter.

Whilst adults have had a lot of experience and learnt many lessons from the experiences of life, we are still green, yet we fail to understand that. The Holy Bible even speaks against pride. It makes it clear that, pride precedes failure. If we could swallow our pride and listen to the little things our elders have for us, we would grow in wisdom. This is because wisdom is like a Baobab tree; so large that no one person's arm can embrace it. It is only by holding hands with others and sharing that we get to know more.

Due to pride, we prefer sharing our ideas and problems with our peers to sharing with our own parents or adults.

Our parents are supposed to be our coaches, mentors and guides. It is common to observe that often, the youth mingle with other young people, and the elderly with the elderly. We need to cross-mingle to tap into their experiences and wisdom. Pride is gradually leading us astray. Pride is robbing us of our great traditions and the knowledge base we need to tap into to truly mature. Many of us are marching into avoidable problems just because of the sort of friends we keep.

To know the road ahead, ask those coming back.

Anonymous

Peer influence

Since we are in the same age group with our peers, it makes it easier and more comfortable to share ideas with them. This could be disastrous. Yet, it's what we prefer to do for many reasons.

We end up being led into the deceitful arms of our less knowledgeable friends whom we confide in. The youth get influenced by the things they see and hear. I remember, during third year in senior high school, we talked about sex a lot. Our mates who had the experience told stories of what they had done, how it felt and flaunted what they had been given by their boyfriends. It was such a wild and interesting conversation that, as soon as they start talking about such things sometimes you began to imagine and yearned so much to give them a try.

Another thing we did was to talk about the guys we met during the holidays; the cute guys we admired so much in and outside the school, new dance styles and many other irrelevant things. We did all these at the expense of our studies. I am sharing these experiences because I want you to keep your head up in order to be focused.

As seniors, we dodged class at times to stay at the dormitory to talk about worthless things. On one of such occasions after hearing the sexual experiences, one of our mates told us about the guy she met during holidays. The champions of the game instantly said the guy loved her. They gave her the green light to go ahead with him. Peer influence had just begun; she grew to like this guy so much within a short period of time as a result of the recommendations of friends.

Her emotions grew so much for him that she could not stay without thinking of him. She made sure she saw his face every holiday. This gave him the chance to start getting closer and closer. Even though she was from a poor home, she would save money to buy call cards and call him on the school's phone booth at least thrice a week.

About two months to write our final exams, she told us the guy was visiting her. That day we were all eager to see his face and see if he was as handsome as she describes him to be. It was a around 3pm and we saw a gentle man neatly dressed in a pair of faded jeans and a long sleeved shirt folded to his elbow. He was in a shiny, well-polished black leather shoes. He had partially tucked in his blue-striped shirt with the top two buttons opened to expose his hairy chest. He had in his hands a flowery-designed polythene bag and you could tell the bag was quite heavy. He walked to a group of us seated under a mango tree and asked for Raina. Instantly we all giggled; we knew it was him and we admired him. We gave him a seat and sent a junior to call Raina from the hostel.

Soon Raina came and they embraced each other, she walked him to a classroom and we saw they walked out with the guy carrying two chairs and Raina holding the poly bag. They sat for hours just talking and we could hear loud rounds of laughter from a distance.

Soon it was getting dark, Raina run to the hostel and brought the bag the guy had brought her. The other ladies jumped on her teasing her and opened the bag. It was loaded with a lot of provisions ranging from powdered chocolate beverage to toiletries. "It is getting late and I am

15

going to see him off", said Raina as she sped off again. In about an hour, she came back to the hostel panting. "What happened?" One of the girls asked probing into why she was panting. She narrated that as she walked him down the road to see him off, before she could say jack he had kissed her so passionately. "That is the first time I was kissed by a man. I just had my first kiss." She broke the news to everyone with so much excitement. This is all because of the psychological preparation she had from peers.

She started describing into details how she felt. They were happy and asked why she didn't go with him when he asked her to. The next day she called him to come over. He took her out and while she was a little tipsy, she happily agreed to go home with him and the unexpected happened. She lost her precious virginity to him.

All these happened because of peer influence, if she had gotten pregnant, she would have dropped out of school. She would be "a born one", as in a woman with a child and no husband. The worst case scenario of this episode would have been her death; especially if the same peers had advised her as friends and influenced her to abort – assuming she had gotten pregnant.

The unfortunate part was her reaction in less than six months after completion, when I personally called her and asked of the guy. She harshly shouted, "That womanizer, I caught him cheating". She now realized he was not worth all the time wasted on him, she just rushed for what she thought was right at a very wrong time.

Be careful not to get influenced into such ugly situations. Out of same peer influences, another friend whom I completed junior high school with dropped out of senior high school during her second year due to pregnancy.

The truth is, there is nothing good in all these things. In the long run you will be the disadvantaged one. What becomes of your dreams, desires, aspirations and plans?

Decision-making

When it comes to making choices as young people, many of us become wobbly. We are unable to make decisions and stand firm by them. We allow other people to make our choices for us. We allow ourselves to be easily influenced by what our friends do, what the media shows to us and even sometimes just what we hear although we have no way of ascertaining its authenticity. We allow our future to be defined by other people's greed and their quest for wealth and fame. We allow people to use us to create their wealth and in turn discourage us from the best way we could make our lives better. This is simply because often times, we feel the urge of wanting to belong, and other times, we feel we need someone to depend on.

Before you ignore all your dreams and start chasing fantasies; mostly what social media portrays to be the real life, ask yourself, "Does this desire complement my talent and my values?" I boarded a vehicle to school one morning with a young man and his sister. They were seated behind me on the back seat. According to him, he had stayed with his aunty and helped in her shop for three years after his senior high school. When he broke the news to her that he wanted to go to a tertiary institution to pursue a programme in nursing, his aunty told him he shouldn't worry because it wouldn't help him, instead she suggested she open a shop for him after he worked for her in a couple more years.

He added that, his aunty said her daughter had been referred several times in the nursing training school so she didn't like the idea of him going to a tertiary institution. She rather advised him to go into business with the promise that she would give him money to deal in different kinds of slippers. She told him about the profitability of business. She said he could use the space in front of her shop and when he got enough money he could rent a store and start the business by himself. If you were this young man, what would you do? Do you think this was the best idea for the young man? What about his dreams and passion for nursing? Should he throw all that away to sell slipper by the roadside? Absolutely not! He wanted to be a graduate; a professional nurse who would heal the sick.

I was stunned when I heard this, because I knew the woman in question so well. She had four children; one was a teacher, another one a nurse and the third in the nursing training college. Her only son was living and working as a nurse abroad. If education was not as good as she claimed, why would all her kids be educated and gainfully employed? This woman was just using her nephew to make money at the expense of his future.

It's time to make decisions for ourselves; decisions that would define our future. If you realize you are at a place where you are not moving forward, don't feel content with it, walk out of it and seek what truly makes you happy. Sometimes, where you stand at the moment may be a comfort zone, but without venturing out there, you wouldn't know the great opportunities that await you. The journey might not be as easy as you would want it to be, but do it anyway. Make sure you get to a position you can be proud of, be able to support yourself and extend your fortunes to help your family and others.

In this 21st Century where technology keeps evolving and multiplying, there will soon be a time when you cannot do any work without professional skill or training. Education is really important even though some people say you don't need education to make it in life. Make the decision to get educated as it will make you a better person in all spheres of life; personal, business, career etc. No matter what path you choose, education gives you the right knowledge, enhances your critical thinking and creativity and causes you to be productive.

Talking of technology especially social media, it is one of the reasons why young people become wobbly. There is too much to choose from, there is always that advert that talks about making quick money and we tend to think that is what life is all about. Don't make social media the scale for checking your success because the poorest person in real life looks the most glamorous on social media.

Your decisions and choices today are the determinants of your value and worth in the near future.

Microwave mentality

The quest to make money and gain fame overnight is what I term microwave mentality. As youth, we want everything quick and fast. Because of what we see and hear around us, we tend to hasten for success. We want to get everything in a twinkle of an eye. The people you see around you, things you hear them say such as "money answers all things; you don't have to go to school to be rich" – all these give us the urge to think of quicker alternatives which could only happen through dubious means.

Gone were the days when if you failed an exam you began to weep bitterly and start chasing remedial classes. These days it's no more like that. Young people don't want to try again when they fail. They find the process of trying again too difficult to go through. Yet they want to progress, they want to do white-collar jobs. In my view, it is simply laziness which leads a lot of them into creating fake results, stealing others' results and using them to get the chance into tertiary institutions. Not only the boys do this, but girls too do it nowadays. The unfortunate thing is, they get caught and dismissed from school.

I want you to embrace the fact that life is not a race; you don't have to rush to create wealth. What you should focus on is creating your inner wealth; character. Your character is what builds your inner and outside beauty. It embodies what gets others closer to you or repel from you. Make sure your focus is not just on making money but growing yourself to be able to sustain the wealth you create. Ensure that any penny you make, you get it in a way that you would be proud to tell everyone about. Make it in a way that you will value and cherish what you have.

The elements of wealth creation are education, resources, opportunity, preparedness and a plan. All these come together to help create wealth. Therefore, if you don't have all these in place, you should know you are not ready and cannot create wealth. There are situations that push us into

21

doing anything at all to create wealth. This could be desperation, jealousy, poverty, and sometimes greed. I want you to accept the fact that nothing changes until you make a change. Not until you make a conscious effort and put in intentional plans, accept the responsibility and fight to attain greatness genuinely; no achievement will come to embrace you. Anything you achieve by dubious means will elude you and be blown away like chaff; you will search but never find it since it's not rooted on solid grounds.

As you try hard to create wealth through the right means, it may be very difficult and slow, but do it anyway; that is how many of the heroes you admire made it. It sets you apart from all others. It is therefore very relevant to be realistic, patient and not be over-ambitious.

The elements of wealth creation are education, resources, opportunity, preparedness and a plan. Don't rush creating wealth, but push for developing your potentials to fit into the career that interests you most; then wealth will chase after you.

Rushing into sexual relationship when unprepared

Another clear problem the youth face is how to manage boy-girl relationships. When I was really young, there were boys I was friends with in my neighborhood. We played, teased each other and had a lot of fun but never thought or did anything sexual. These days, it's the opposite; young people are just desperate to explore their sexuality. This often leads to unexpected, unwanted and inevitable pregnancies. If you come from a family where your needs are always met and you never lack anything, walk to your parents, embrace and thank them for the great sacrifices put into making your life comfortable. Appreciate them for the planning and work they had to put in to enable you to be happy today. On the other hand, if you are from families where your parents are struggling to take care of your needs and you never get three square meals a day, unable to buy your books, pay your fees etc. then pick a cue from that.

You might be suffering today because of the negligence or ignorance of your parents. A few mistakes my dad made some years ago brought a lot of struggles to my siblings and me. I had to literally become a mother to two teenage girls, as I mentioned in the earlier chapter, all because of their impatience and haste. How do you want your family to be? What kind of life do you envisage for yourself and your children? Being sexually active at a young age, when care is not taken, can lead to a whole lot of complexities.

Many girls from poor homes tend to think that relationship and marriage are the panacea to poverty. They don't know what love is or isn't; they submit their emotions to men who tend to care less for them. Some of these men actually take advantage of the needs of these girls and use them for their selfish gains. Before you think about a sexual relationship, assess yourself; finances, dreams, career, and the responsibilities that come with it, especially when you become a mother. Ask yourself; is this boy aware of the responsibilities of fatherhood? Is he capable of caring for himself, talk less of raising a child?

Today we see beautiful young girls who are very intelligent drop out of school to take up responsibilities they are unprepared for; motherhood. The question is, can opposite sexes still be friends and not engage in sexual immoralities? Yes! This is highly possible. It is all about seeking safety and purity of the persons we claim to love. We have to be patient and do what is necessary before thinking of what is fun to do. For a religious person, I will like to remind you of what God, our creator expects of us; to love our neighbors as ourselves. We should go into relationships with the motive of bringing the best out of the other person not with a hidden agenda; "What can he do for me?" "What can I get from her?" Take away your personal pleasure and seek to please God. Let your actions, choices and decisions be focused on pleasing God and adding value to other people.

In your quest for friendship, your goals should focus on being an exception. Choose friends because you truly care about each other and are ready to sacrifice your pleasure and lust to make the other pure and great.

The other form of relationship common among the youth these days is "Sugar Daddy or Mummy". What will make a young lady or a young man decide to be with a person of the opposite sex who is old enough to be his or her grandparent? The answer is simple – MONEY. Poverty is causing many young people to sell their bodies for wealth. It has now turned into a butter system; I give you money, you in turn give yourself to me to satisfy my lust. Don't forget, not many people give gifts for free; no matter how long it takes, they will take something back in return for what they had given you.

Love, I know, is a tender feeling of affection, faithfulness, commitment and trust for someone. Love is not a trade; it is sincerity, it is not an obligatory; it is freedom. Love feels no regret, rejection or insufficiency so if you feel any of these things, know you are in the wrong place, with the wrong person at the wrong time! Love is simple, not complicated. So if you are young and beautiful, handsome and energetic, and you find yourself in a position that is pushing you into marketing yourself to survive, you might want to rethink your decision.

True love is without any strings attached, and before that can happen, you must be self-reliant, independent and very ready in all areas of life. Without these, you would find yourself in the arms of a person who needs you for only one reason; sex. He or she lures you into bed untimely and all your conversations are always around money or sex.

I want to share with you what I did to provide my needs in the most humbling way devoid of men. I was ready to do any job I could find no matter how demeaning, less-paying or tiring it was so long as I made a genuine income. I remember back at college I borrowed a camera and went into photography to sustain myself at school. On some occasions, I prepared shito (a pepper sauce mostly used by students) for sale. Whenever I was on holidays, I would bring fruits from my father's farm at the village to sell in the city by hawking in the hot sun so I could make money. If your parents are traders, you can be of great help to them as well. Don't mind what your friends may say; they may be mocking you today, but with your target at heart and in mind, be persistent. They will come begging you some day when you had risen to the top through all the hassles.

When I completed junior high school, I was selling in my aunty's store and there was this elderly man with a very different accent who came to buy from us. Whenever he came, he wanted me to serve him. He admired me because according to him, I spoke very good English. He became a very good friend of ours. One day, he invited me to his house to meet his beautiful wife. He started asking lots of questions and got to know I completed Junior High

School the same year as his daughter. He asked of my grades and I told him I had not gone for my results because I owed some school fees. He gave me money to pay the fees and collect my results. When he visited the shop the next time, I showed him the results and he was so proud of me and mentioned I did better than his daughter who went to a very good school in Accra.

This man took me as his child and kept providing my needs and promised to finance my education in the senior high school. Even though he wasn't able to fulfil his promise because he had to travel abroad with his family, I can never forget him.

I still remember him every day and cherish him for his encouragement and faith in me. His compassion, love and genuine kindness got me fired up to become better. If an older man of his age could inspire and support me without looking for anything in return, then what are you doing with that sugar daddy or mummy asking for sex from you? He or she is the exact opposite of the man I have just described. Such older men or women care less about you; they only want to satisfy their sexual desires. Don't let them use you! Please cut them off.

Anyone who isn't ready to help you genuinely is not worth keeping around. Sometimes, it is sad that our parents push us into some of these relationships. Remember life is not just about today, there is tomorrow. Remember, you will face the consequences alone should anything go wrong.

Anita, a friend of mine, had an experience which was the exact opposite of mine. After senior high school, she did not pass all her papers just like me, yet she wanted to go to the nurses' training school. A friend suggested to her to approach a well-to-do man in her vicinity for support. It was believed that this man could help her gain admission into Ho Nursing Training School.

When she approached him, he agreed to help her. This got her very excited and hopeful. In a week's time, he asked her to travel with him to Ho where he worked so that he could introduce her to his friend who was the vice principal of the nursing training school. Due to his influence in society, she trusted and had so much respect for him. She followed him to the city very excited and thankful that finally, her dreams were coming true. When they arrived in the city, he took her to a hotel room and had sex with her forcefully. She couldn't scream or do anything because everyone watched her walk in willingly. At the end of it all, the man had sex with her and never helped her. She returned to town in tears and shared the sad experience with me. She could not report to the police or talk to her mother about it. Be very careful the sort of people you confide in for help; they may just want to take advantage of you. Even though not all people are like that, you never know who is, since it's not written on anyone's forehead.

Relationships are meant to help, not to destroy, to love not to kill and to be enjoyed not endured. Only enter into a real relationship when you are independent, ready and capable of handling the consequences.

CHAPTER THREE

SMASH THE BEDROCK OF FEAR DEEP INSIDE

Setbacks are not defeat; bounce back onto your feet!

I learnt a great lesson from my exam results. There was no doubt that the school I attended had many logistical deficiencies; insufficient textbooks, few teachers and lack of tools for practical experiments. Most of the time, we studied on our own since we had few or no teachers to handle some key subjects, such as mathematics and science. These were factors that I would say contributed to my failure. Nevertheless, I could have done better if I had put in more effort than I did.

With all these at the back of my mind, I was more determined to pass my remedial classes once and for all. I had understood the saying that, "once bitten twice shy."

The problems we face most times teach us priceless lessons we live with for the rest of our lives.

Eventually, the date was due for the private exam and we wrote the papers. Can you imagine the outcome under the pressures of taking care of my siblings and teaching? To my utmost surprise, I failed beautifully again. My result slip was decorated with two F's and one E. This was because there was no adequate preparation before the exams. It was a very colorful failure; you could imagine the extra agony and sorrow I went through. I got to a higher stage of breakdown. I call this point *"paralysis"*.

I began to ask questions like, "Why me? So all these prayers didn't work? "All the burning of candles didn't pay off? Why did I fail again? Why am I not progressing?" I saw no improvement or change in my results at all. The real frustration began to weigh me down. I came to a halt and really lost focus. I decided to just sit and watch what would happen next. Life meant nothing to me anymore. The thought of going back to square one and starting classes all over again gave me a terrible headache. I couldn't hold myself from crying for several days. I started thinking, "Is it a curse in this family that no one goes up the ladder beyond senior high school?" Then I remembered my grandfather was a head teacher in a basic school. So, I wondered, "Am I blockheaded? Is God really watching all I am going through?"

Reluctantly, I began to drift away; I shied away from church and the company of friends. I wanted to be alone. I stayed indoors most of the time just crying. All those times, I knew that education meant everything to me since I didn't have the strength to do any form of manual labor and this brought much more pain. I thought God was being unfair to me, and I decided to quit. Are you in such a situation and feel like giving up? Do not worry. You are not being tempted by God but rather, you are being tested to develop endurance. Hold on fast because help is on the way.

Challenges are often the forces that push us to go beyond the limit we set for ourselves.

You need to know that setbacks are not defeat; they only delay you a little bit. You can still bounce back to your feet with determination. Every great person you see today had setbacks; unforeseen occurrences brought them down. Yet, they were able to surmount them. That contributed to all the goodness you admire about them and desire to be or have. You can only be it, if you are ready to see your setbacks as trials, not defeat.

Hold on to your courageous self

In all these afflictions, there was this part of me that yearned so much to go back to school; to have a higher education and have a better life. This is what gave me my strength. It restored the lost optimism; it rearranged my thoughts and revitalized me to move on. I wanted to be happy, I desired to be self-reliant and I gravely desired a better life; a life different from what I was born into and grew up knowing. I wanted the life I saw my neighbors enjoy with their kids, which I never had. This is where I found the courage, and challenged myself daily to be better through the right means; hard work, persistence perseverance and sacrifices.

When you are faced with such difficulties and feel like there is nothing to live for, what do you do? Do you just sit back and watch? Do you just cry and yell or you rather find another way out before it gets too late? There is this saying that goes "Make hay while sun shines." Are you doing exactly that? Or you are relaxed and living on assumptions and not actions? In such times, don't let your mind communicate impossibilities; that negative energy can discourage you. Believe and think that you can lift yourself up from the shackles. Remember your target, dreams and the change you are gravely yearning for and kick start your passion to attain them.

Often times, during anguish and distress, we turn to feel we are not good enough. We begin to look down on ourselves. Once you begin to have a negative self-image, you begin to feel unworthy of everything and of course you cannot give what you do not have.

Sometimes you feel you have the least or no place in this world just because you have been made to believe so. The worst is that, the thought of suicide could even begin crawling into your mind. Do not allow difficult situations to make you think this way. You are the driver of your life, keep controlling the car, which is your mind. Don't let your emotions rule over you. Remember those hard times are only temporary and will soon change.

I took another bold step: went back to do the remedial class and started all over again. Amazingly, I began to see some of the old faces I had taken the exams with. Then I paused, "Wait a minute! So they also couldn't make it?" I learnt something here and I want to share it with you. I realized my problems were far less than others'. There is this song that says, "Someone wishes to be like you". This is so true! Minimize the way you tell people about your problems, eliminate the attitude of comparing yourself to others who have made it. So long as you have life, you have what it takes to elevate yourself to the next level.

Be glad that you are alive and at least you have been able to take a step ahead of others. Pick inspiration from those who are ahead of you, see them as examples of where you would love to be. Do not compare yourself to them, or else you will end up losing hope and give up. Always find consolation in the fact that despite your condition, you are still ahead of others. After all, others aren't where you are yet. This is why you should do it again, you have to try it again, you may win this time round and this is what should spur you on. You may not know where life takes you, but never give up until you win.

This was my experience and the lesson learnt. With this, my heart began to settle down. I began to realize that I was not alone. I was not the only one with such depressing problems. Even though solitude weighed me down, there were others in the same boat like me; they shared the same fate as me. I gathered courage and got this conviction that I could make a change in my grades provided that I could make another sacrifice of time and energy. It's true you have lost time, money and more but everything could be restored in thousand folds provided you are ready to make more sacrifices of your play time, leisure, sleep time and re-channel your energy into achieving your dream.

Miraculously, all the doubts that I had about myself began to fade gradually. I started regaining my strength and the edge to move on. As I started chatting and mingling with other colleagues, I realized that my problem was lighter than that of others; they poured their sad hearts out in our conversations. At least I passed one out of the three papers I wrote but others got absolutely nothing from the eight papers they had written. This signifies that, sometimes we think we are the only ones going through rough moments until we hear of others' condition.

When the walls that surround you are silent and solitude weighs like a stone. As you search for a shoulder to lean on, remember you are not alone.

David Prowse-

35

I had a friend, who was a very good student during the junior high school days, but after JHS we lost contact. One day as I was walking through town, we bumped into each other. Having a conversation with her, I realized she had gone through worse experiences. Sena never gave up on education even though she got pregnant, dropped out of high school and became a laughing stock among her friends and relatives. She picked up the pieces and began to mend them together.

First, she gathered courage and went back to SHS to join the second year students. That was how a great opportunity met her preparation and turned her life around. She got a scholarship to participate in an exchange program for one year in the United States of America. After completion of the exchange program, she came back to Ghana and wrote private senior high school exam administered by the West African Examination Council which she passed. She progressed to study for her Bachelor's Degree in Medical Technology and Healthcare Science with which she is currently practicing as a Medical Technologist in United States.

She got these opportunities when she went back to school two years after the birth of her child. She boldly overcame the stigma that resulted from negative rumors. The most amazing thing was that she didn't return to the same high school to re-write her exams when she returned from the United States; she just opted for the non-school private exams.

If she had not held herself together, put the past behind her and forged ahead, she would not have gotten this far. You can do anything you set your mind to do no matter how long it may take. There is no life without setbacks but what you make out of it is what is most relevant.

One of the courageous things you can do is to identify yourself, know who you are, what you believe in, and where you want to go.

Sheila Murray Bethel

I triumphed over misery, you too can!

Those days, whenever I set my eyes on my friend who had the chance to go to the teacher training school through the first access course opportunity, I asked, "When will I also be like her?" The thought that I had to stay home for one whole year was really a big blow to me. But I didn't let that weigh me down. I encouraged myself all the time by saying, "I can be like her only if I take the pain to work a little harder". I continued the remedial classes with the certainty that I must get there too.

After closing from my basic school teaching job one afternoon, I set off to classes. On my way, I met a friend, Angela who informed me that access course forms for Teacher Training College were out. I went with her to St Theresa's College of Education to check for the requirements on the notice board. To my dismay, it required five passes with aggregate twenty-one or six passes with aggregate twenty-seven. I became so confused because I had five passes with aggregate twenty-two. Just because of one difference, I was on the verge of losing another chance. At that juncture, I decided to take the chance and applied anyway. I went and bought the forms, filled it out and submitted it at the appropriate place. I waited patiently to be called to start the six-week intensive training.

After a month and a few weeks later, I heard the list was out for selected candidates. They were to report and start the six-week intensive training after which they would take a final exam. The qualified ones would then be posted to various teacher training colleges. I went to the notice board to check if I was among the selected ones. When I got there, everybody was rejoicing and I was excited too. I started checking for my name. I searched from top to bottom, side to side but never found it. Tears started flowing down my cheeks when I realized what I dreaded had come true. I left the scene to avoid any notice from other candidates who were checking theirs too. I was really hurt and angry. Even though I knew I wasn't qualified, I was expecting a. miracle due to what I thought was a negligible margin of variation from the minimum threshold.

I got home feeling very weak and sick. I couldn't do anything at all and I had lost appetite for food. I felt the food was bitter in my mouth. The last thing I remembered doing that day was praying in my sleep to God that He knows my needs, He knows why I needed to go to school that year; I wept and wept till sleep took me away.

When you get weak in the midst of trials, the enemy gets the strength to overcome you.

The next morning I woke up, did my chores and dressed up. I took my two results slips and went to the school's premises again. When I got there I happened to meet the Vice Principal of the College. I gathered courage and approached him. I showed my results to him told him everything. He listened quietly until I was done; then he asked, "What is your total aggregate?"

"Five passes with 22 twenty-two", I replied. He looked at me keenly and said to my face, "Oh ok, I see. There is nothing I can do. You are not qualified, that's why you weren't selected. Try next year." Wow! What a shock? I was thinking there could be a miracle; I was thinking God would make a way where there was no way.

What would you do if it were you? I just said "Thank you" and left his sight. Your oppressors will never leave you till they see you are out dated, useless and of no value. In such situations, we need to go on our knees and call on God to intervene. At that point, only the power of God could propel you forward. The worst of all is how some people in authority take advantage of such conditions and get ignorant, young, desperate and beautiful poor girls to bed. Their only aim is to satisfy their lust and they end up not willing to fulfill their promises. I gave an example of this situation in Angela's story.

Miracles come into fulfillment with our effort; you have to take a step of faith for God to take action of making your dreams visible.

I want to share with you a friend's experience with one of such users. Suzy told me about a new filling station she was hoping to get a job at. I was so happy for her and called her at dawn and taught her how to prepare her C.V. I also guided her to write an application letter. She did everything right, sent them for typing, printed them out and submitted the application. She was called for interview and afterwards, one of the panelists asked her to wait behind. At the end, the interviewer took her number and said she will hear from him.

40

I was home one afternoon when she called me and said the man asked her to meet him at a hotel. I suspected what his intentions were and told her to be very careful. I asked her to act nice but be very assertive and never get into a hotel room if he asks her to. When she returned, she told me the man was the manager of the filling station. He said he really liked her the moment he laid eyes on her and wanted her to be his girlfriend. He promised to give her everything and make her happy. My gracious God! When she poured out those words I was really shocked and angry.

According to her, this man was wearing a wedding ring. She believed he might even have children.

Some people can be heartless. In someone's desperate need of a job to help her make a decent living and survive, the man wanted her to satisfy his sexual desires. When you come across such people be smart to avoid them. You are worth much more than any amount of money. If you lose that opportunity, as Suzy did, the right time will eventually come with the right opportunity. Don't sell yourself cheap.

I am citing all these examples to emphasize that life is not easy. It is not a bed of roses; you've got to work persistently hard and smart to make a way. You may be humiliated, insulted and disgraced, but don't let it weigh you down. You need to gather courage, keep pushing assiduously; that's how you can rise above all these

41

tribulations. Always know your vision and keep working hard towards achieving them, but never allow anyone to use your needs as a trap. You deserve better.

You are not anointed to run the race that people tell you to run but anointed to run the race that God has called you to run.

- Our Daily Manna-

Do you know that words have power? The words people use on us have the potential to ruin or make us. That is another element of distraction you need to run away from. I will advise you not to take what others say about you as the truth; it is just their thought. Don't give others the chance to determine your level of success. Prove yourself above their thoughts and beliefs about you; that is the way to overcome unhappiness. My dear, remember, quitters never win and winners never quit no matter how fierce the battle is.

When I got home, I thought through the words of the vice principal, "You are not qualified, that's why you were not selected." I wondered what happens if I'm unable to go to school that year. In anger, I said to myself, "I will go there till I am granted the opportunity to take part in the course".

42

The next morning, I dressed neatly and walked to the school again. On my way, I was rehearsing what I would say if I happened to meet the coordinator in charge of the access course. I walked briskly to the school's administration and this time, I saw a lady seated behind a desk. I presumed she was the secretary. I asked her where I could find the coordinator in charge of the course. The lady directed me to a room directly opposite where she was seated. I knocked and entered. My heart jumped into my mouth when I realized it was the same man from the previous day. My heart was racing so fast and I nearly landed on the ground.

Holding the same files and shivering vigorously, I greeted him and he asked me to sit. "How may I help you?" He asked. It was obvious then that he couldn't make me out. "I applied for the course but was not selected", I said, handing over the documents to him. He looked at the name and looked at my face. "Have we met before?" He asked. "Are you not the same person who came here yesterday?" He persisted. "Yes sir, I am the one", I responded in fear. "I said you are not qualified, that's why you were not picked. What do you want me to do? Why do you want to make my work very difficult?" He yelled. "Go back home, this is not your time, try next year". I was really embarrassed and left his sight in shame.

All I could think of was how to manage and get home in one piece. At this point my last strong hope was blown away. Tears could not find its way out any more; I was just speechless. No word from any one could change my mind, convince me or calm me down anymore. No amount of motivation from my dad could save the situation. I got into the room and locked myself up until my sisters came back from school. I stayed indoors for five days and refused to eat.

This proves the fact that what people say to us at a point in time can either bring our spirit down or even ruin our future. The manner in which some people present issues to us or communicate to us could have adverse effect on our lives. All along, my younger sisters were following all that was happening to me because of the state in which I was. They were both very sad; no one to joke and dance for them to laugh, no one to talk to them. I was really depressed and sunk into seclusion.

On the fifth day of staying indoors without eating well, my sisters secretly called my dad on a neighbor's phone and told him what was happening. My dad called and tried to convince me to move on and get the best out of the exams. Later in the afternoon, one of my sisters came back to me and said, "I think you should try again for the last time. Then you know that you have done your very best." I heard her but pretended I didn't hear what she said.

There was only one word in all her sentence that woke up my persistence. The word "best" got me thinking. I wondered if I had done enough on this issue. At first, I didn't really mind her because my mind was made up until she queried my commitment to myself. Before this awakening, I had accepted my fate. Throughout the weekend, I had so many thoughts; what do I have to lose if I go back to check again? What do I stand to lose if I don't make it to school? I started comparing both consequences.

On Monday morning when I realized they were all gone out, I got out of bed, prepared and headed out with my documents. I went to the compound this time hoping for a positive result. Amazingly, as soon as I got to the school, I saw a group of students seated under some mango trees. I walked to them and asked if they knew where I could go to sort out issues about my name not appearing on the list. "Oh ok, we also have the same problem and we were told to wait here for the coordinator himself", one of them responded. After waiting for about an hour, we saw a lady walking towards our direction. I made her out since I saw her the previous time at the administration. She came to us and said, "My name is Rita; I'm the secretary of the principal of the school. I will take you all to the coordinator of the program. He arrived today and will meet you in a few minutes. Please come with me."

45

She took us to one of the bungalows and gave us a seat. She turned to me and said "I have seen you on two occasions being confronted by the Vice Principal, what was the problem?" After telling her my plight, she quickly took my results, calculated the grades and said, "Some people came here with same problems yesterday and the coordinator allowed them to join; let's hope he allows you too." I felt very relieved. I began to smile, brightened up and kept praying for good news. Knowing that this is the last chance, I trusted God to intervene and decide my fate. I looked up and said, "God if it is your will, let me be granted the opportunity."

I know you are wondering what the outcome was, but before I come to that, I want to say one thing. Lou Holtz said, *"I think everyone should experience defeat once during their career. They will learn a lot from it"*. I will say everyone should experience hardship in life and this will help them learn a lot and develop a heart of patience and empathy for others. This was what happened to me. I learned how to hold on in hard times and never give up. It also shaped how I view and treat people who are striving to make life meaningful.

The coordinator finally walked onto the porch with a broad smile. "Oh Secretary, you are here, how may I be of help to you?" He asked. Sister Rita handed over my result slip to him and said my sister is having same problems as the others and I was wondering if you could take a look at it for them. The man took the results and pulled out a pen from his pocket. He sat down on a chair beside a writing desk and started writing some things on a piece of paper. After about three minutes, he said, "You got English Language and Science but did not get Mathematics?" "Yes sir", I replied quickly. Then he said, "The requirement is five passes with twenty-one". Then my heart started pounding faster because that had always been the basis for my rejection. He continued, "You have five passes with aggregate twenty-two instead of twenty-one but *I WILL NOT DENY YOU THIS OPPORTUINITY.* Go for your things and join your colleagues and **prove** yourself". Wow! What a relief! I was more than happy. I started shedding tears of joy.

I was denied on two occasions just to be accepted by the coordinator himself? Amazing! What would you have done if it were you? How many times would you have tried? For anything good to happen, there must be an undying zeal to see its fruition and fulfillment. There is the need for follow-up and consistency over time even when you fail. That is how you learn new ways of doing the same thing.

God's time is the best and he does all things in his own apt time. Sometimes, God puts a comma in our lives just to test our level of endurance, perseverance and ability to trust him. Comma literally means take a little rest in a sentence; meaning there is more to come to complete that particular sentence.

So God puts a comma just to show that there is more to come but often, we turn the comma into a full stop. We feel the world has denied us what we need and therefore stop trying. Don't get tempted to hurriedly put full stops at points where God only wants us to wait a while. What do you think would have happened if I had given up on the very first trial? I would have stayed at home crying endlessly all to no avail, and perhaps I would have stayed home for several more years. I would have wasted time and lost the opportunity prepared for me. And as I speak, that access course was the very last one that was ever organized for students to access teacher training colleges.

God has given you the ability to endure tough times and you need to make use of it. As a youth, you need to make a little more sacrifice and persevere; that's the difference between winners and losers. Hassles, miseries, difficulties and more will always keep coming but with a positive attitude, you will overcome them.

To be able to pave a way through the hassles, you must be intentionally persistent, be positive and learn to sacrifice. Don't take what others say as final, but what you truly want. Keep it in mind that life is a journey; it is only then that you will have guts to fight till the end.

CHAPTER FOUR

THE POWER OF DETERMINATION

Be determined to be a victor

I read a story about a great man and I want to share with you. He is my best example whenever I talk about determination. As a little boy, he had a job of going to school early to start the fire in the country schoolhouse to warm the room before his teacher and his classmates arrive.

One morning they arrived to meet the schoolhouse engulfed in flames, with the boy trapped in there. They dragged the little boy out and took him to the nearby hospital. He had major burns at the lower half of his body. From his sick bed dreadfully burnt, he heard the doctor telling his mum he was going to die no matter what they did due to the severity of the burns. But the brave boy didn't want to die. He made up his mind he wants to survive and his system accepted that psychologically. He started recovering to the surprise of all the doctors.

Another day, he overheard the doctor telling his mum that he would be a cripple for life, and it would almost be better if he had died. Once more, the brave boy made up his mind; he would walk again. Eventually, he was

49

discharged and taken home. Everyday his mother would massage his little legs, but there was no feeling, no control, nothing. Yet his determination that he would walk again was as strong as ever. When he wasn't in bed, he was confined in a wheelchair.

One sunny day, his mother wheeled him out into the yard to get some fresh air. This day, instead of sitting there, he threw himself from the chair to the ground. He pulled himself across the grass dragging his legs behind him. He worked his way to a white picket fence bordering their lot. With great effort, he raised himself up on the fence. Then skate by skate, he began dragging himself along the fence, resolved that he would walk. He started to do that every day until he achieved a smooth path all around the yard beside the fence. There was nothing he wanted more than to develop life in those legs again.

Amazingly, through his daily massages, with his iron persistence and his resolute determination, he did develop the ability to stand, walk haltingly, then to walk on his own and then to run. He began to walk to school, then to run to school, to run for the sheer joy of running. Later in college, he made the track team. Later in Madison Square Garden, this young man who was not expected to survive and would surely not walk again, could never hope to run, run the world's fastest mile. His name was Dr. Glenn Cunningham.

If life can be restored to dead cells and tissues, if someone who was condemned to become a cripple could walk again, just as a result of determination and hard work, then what is it that you cannot do if you are determined? Determination is a great tool we all need. Determination fuels you when all other things like your environment, family and financial status fail to urge you on. Your determination comes from how serious you are to attain your objectives. Like Dr. Cunningham, be very optimistic about your situation. Always find something good to hold on to even when life is failing you. He was in severe pain, yet his mind, body and soul believed and trusted that he could sail through and yes, he did. You can do it too my dear.

Everything can be taken from a man but one thing: the last of human freedoms to choose one's own way.

Viktor Frankl

You don't have the power to decide what happens to you in the next minute, but you have the power to choose what you make out of it. You have the freedom to think, dream and wish for all you desire, but without hard work and determination, it will remain only a desire.

Explore possible ways out of the hassles

"Twenty years from now you will be more disappointed by the things that you didn't do than by the ones you did do. So throw off the

bowlines. Sail away from the safe harbor. Catch the trade winds in your sails. Explore. Dream. Discover."

- Mark Twain

I want you to take a look at the three powerful words Mark Twain used in the above quote; "explore", "dream" and "discover".

Explore means to delve into something, to study, survey, search, learn or discover something. An explorer is a person who travels to distant and unknown places to find out more about them. The only things that can take an explorer through his or her quest to discover new things are courage, passion and perseverance. Without these three things it will be very difficult to be an explorer.

The best time to explore the great opportunities available to you is while you are still young. This will enable you to discover your abilities and equip yourself with the requisite skills, knowledge and expertise to take you to higher heights. Your ability to exercise this skill will contribute to the quality of your life in the near future. Are you the exploring kind or one who coils up in a shell of complain and self-pity? Or are you there saying, "I have no one to help me"?

Life is difficult for everyone and the economy is very rigid, so it is very difficult to find people who will keep giving you support daily. What you need is someone who gives you daily encouragement, guidance or teaches you how to earn a living. The rest is your responsibility. A person who teaches you how to fish is worth more than the one giving you fish each day. What happens if he or she is no more? If you meet someone who has the ability and willingness to help you, ask for a lasting solution not short-term or temporary stuffs.

Some people say one does not necessarily have to go to school to make it in life but I stand to differ because education helps you in diverse ways. It helps you to read and write, it opens your understanding and connects you to greater opportunities. Education has the ability to inculcate new skills; the use of technology and how to communicate properly. Assess yourself and know what you love to do and find ways to maximize them.

You also have to check yourself; get to know your talents. Some people are multitalented; if you are one of such people, go further to find out which of your talents dominates the rest of them. Identify which of them is easy-going, fun and you can use without any stress. Now get to work by putting that talent into action; that could be your way out of the hassle. Some people are great today because they were able to identify, add value to and work out their talents. You can also get something much more from your talent if you could do the same.

Heroes stand out because they find another way at every dead end and an opportunity in all impossibility.

Have a dream; love greatness!

Let's now take a look at the next word Twain used; Dream! Dream here simply implies something that someone hopes for, longs for or is ambitious about. It is usually something difficult to attain or far removed from your present circumstances. Dreaming is having the mental picture of what you wish to make out of your life. The things we hope to become are our dreams. The mental pictures we have of people we admire are our dreams.

You must have a dream; this dream is what will give you the drive to go on until you arrive at the peak and still keep climbing. It gives you the strength of endurance because you start to think and imagine yourself at the stage you always desire. Many great people we hear about today had dreams; dreams that scared them to the core.

Through resilience they worked tirelessly to give birth to these dreams. They had in mind something great to achieve and worked hands-on. They imagined it in their minds, believed and trusted it with their hearts, and worked it out with their hands and body.

Finally, with the spirit of perseverance, it became their reality. Their dreams propelled them to move even in times when their feet told them, "No, you can't go on, you are tired". They worked harder when their body experienced severe pains and needed rest. Yet their words were, "I must get there".

Let's take a look at Martin Luther King Junior who experienced real difficult situations; segregation, threats, violence, racism etc. He still had a dream and that gave him hope for the future. He said, "I have a dream that one day this nation will rise up and live out the true meaning of its creed... we hold this truth to be self-evident, that all men are created equal... I have a dream that my four little kids will one day live in a nation where they will not be judged by the colour of their skin but by the content of their character".

Amazingly, he is dead and gone, but America stands as the true result of his dream and what he worked so hard for. Now you can see people from different races and religions regarded as one people – Americans. They all have equal rights and enjoy opportunities. Life without a dream is a life without any direction and a life without direction leads you to a dead end. Without aims in our lives, we only struggle to exist, not to live.

The path we take may be shaky and cruel, but the world is waiting for that unique contribution each of us is born to make for the betterment of this world.

Add value to your talent and resources

Many of us have desires so great yet we have no knowledge of how to get there. Others have added value to their lives yet they don't know how to handle and sustain what they have attained. Some have all they need to accelerate into greatness, but they don't value it, others who don't have, rather value it; this is human nature.

In this regard, we can categorize the youth of today into three groups. First, those who have wealthy parents, yet they don't value education. The other group comprises those whose parents have absolutely nothing yet they do value education and wish to go as high as life could take them. The final group has the ones who have nothing yet do nothing to educate themselves. They do not see education as a way to transform their lives and family. They seem content with the poor conditions they live in. They seem satisfied with the hardship they face daily.

Sometimes, those who have all the resources at their disposal rather take things for granted when they should take it more seriously instead. They feel life will never change, but it's a big lie. Is this how you were ten years ago? You were not like this. You looked younger and were less knowledgeable than you are now.

This means change has taken place and change is inevitable in our lives. There are different kinds of changes; financial, health, educational etc. No matter how rich you are, your finances can change, due to ill-health or something else. This is why you always need to be prepared and plan for unforeseen occurrences.

Many of us have great talents, yet we don't make use of them. Perhaps you can sing, dance, run, or talk to convince people but all these talents can fade away if you don't add value to them. The value you add to your talent is the education you get and the training you sign up for to attain mastery of that talent.

Imagine two people looking for a job and they both have the talent to sing. One had been training his voice and has done studies into all kinds of music genre while learning how to play some musical instruments. The other does no training, has no knowledge of the various genres and can't play any musical instrument yet they had the same results in an examination and have equally good voice quality. My question now is, "Which of these people would you employ in a music studio"? "Which of them do you think would be given admission to a music school"?

I made mention that I had to find a pupil-teaching job after senior high school. This really helped me a lot when, as part of the requirement at the teacher training school, we had to do teaching practice. My prior experience came in handy but for many of my colleagues, standing in front of a class to teach was a nightmare since it was their first time.

On the issue of sacrifice, I have worked at a radio station for six years as a volunteer. I had no pay or salary, yet I hosted three programmes; one of which I designed on my own. I was always busy going up and down and spent my own money whenever the need arose.

Now I have work experience as a radio presenter. I started presenting one program which was my own initiative but due to my hard work, sacrifice, dedication and punctuality, I was given two other programs to host. How can this experience help elevate my dreams of becoming a journalist? With a testimonial from my former radio station, I am likely to be offered a job at another radio station anywhere else in the country.

My work experience can cause me to be employed over someone who just completed a radio school without any form of experience. This will definitely create an opportunity for me if I want to join another radio station at any point in time.

Even if you are home awaiting your result, please search for a job to acquire some skills and techniques as experience. These skills are the values you are gradually adding to your talent, and you will never regret doing it even if you do it for free.

The value you add to your talent makes you marketable. Likewise, the resources at your disposal might not be much, but when value is added it brings so much benefit

Learn to adjust to complex situations

Difficult conditions we face are just there to test our pulse. They are to see how ready we are to face the real troubles ahead. For us to be able to overcome difficulties and survive, we must learn to adjust. Keep it in mind that these situations are not here to stay forever; they are just conditions which will definitely come to pass.

Let's look at this scenario: You have a budget of GHC 500 while all you earn is GHC 300; how are you going to survive on that? The first thing to do is to adjust your budget. Do well to live within your means and your needs. To do this, sit down and put your items under two categories: *needs* and *wants*. Needs are things you can't survive without and wants are those you can live without. Even under needs, you have those that are *urgent* and those that are *not urgent*. When you classify them you can now sort out the very necessary items to form your budget.

What are you trying to do here? You are trying to adjust to the situation; you are cutting down cost in order to live within your means and meet your needs.

Adjustment is necessary for our daily survival as youth. At the point where there was nothing I could do and nowhere to go, I made an adjustment to be able to live and still feel comfortable without my aunty. I told myself, "Life must go on". Don't always wait to be taken care of, dare to do that yourself. I adjusted in different ways. I maintained and kept my old clothes clean. I managed the only church sandals I had and wore slippers almost everywhere I went. At that time, I considered all those things as wants; without new ones, I could still survive.

Sometimes, one must forgo even food to be able to achieve an aim. This is something I have done on several occasions. There were times I had to give the only money I had to my sisters to pay their exam fees and we would cook without fish.

You don't get in life what you want but what you are willing to give. In order to move forward in success it's so important to know who you are, where you come from and where you want to be. It is important to know what your foundation is; the kind of family you are born into - rich, average or poor. This helps you to understand your parents' situation. It enables you to have a high sense of contentment and willingness to compromise and endure the hardship you face now and to enjoy the good fortune in your future. This is what is termed as delayed gratification.

He who knows no hardships will know hardihood. He who faces no certainty will need courage. — *Myslerious Kongle*

CHAPTER FIVE

THE REWARD OF PERSEVERANCE

I persevered for a better life.

Growing up, I've always wanted to be a fashion designer. I was successful in my junior high school final exams and went to a good senior high school. I completed with five passes without math and science. I decided to learn dressmaking from a roadside dressmaker while I continued to write my private exams.

I established my own little dress-making shop in my bedroom. I had many customers as time went by. I chose to write and rewrite the private exam year after year for five solid years. I was determined to pass my mathematics and science in order to continue my education at the polytechnic. I told myself, "I will not stop until I pass the exams", and kept on doing my sewing as I learnt styles and techniques from friends, magazines and online.

The worst part of all my struggles was that I kept meeting younger people who used to be in the same shoes with me but had passed the exams and moved on to tertiary institutions. People gossiped so much about me. Some said I was block-headed, others said I was good for nothing and would remain a seamstress in my bedroom forever. The more I heard what they said, the more I felt a strong urge to prove them wrong. "I will definitely pass these papers and go to the polytechnic", I told myself always. My mum who is a "kenkey" (a local food made from fermented corn) seller told me nothing good comes easily and that I should not give up on her and myself. She promised to continue selling kenkey till I become what I wanted to be.

The day I was going to write the sixth time, I told myself, "This is my last time; I have gathered enough knowledge about writing this mathematics and science, and now I will not fail again". That day, I came out of the exams hall feeling very bold. I made a B in science and a C in mathematics.

With this I was able to get the opportunity to enter the polytechnic and studied fashion. I found it super easy because, I had a formidable knowledge base in it from the training I had received from the roadside seamstress and other sources. I graduated with a second class and now I own a fashion enterprise. I am now self-employed, independent and able to assist my family in diverse ways.

Philomena A.

Motivation

Whenever someone told me I was not good enough, I always saw that as a challenge. I had this inherent motivation, a motivation that comes from within me. I also think the kind of people I saw in my neighborhood growing up gave me a lot to tap inspiration from. I got the chance to see what a better life looked like even though I could not experience it then. I compared what I saw daily to what my reality was and I knew I wanted a different reality.

I lived in a neighborhood where there were lots of government workers, mostly teachers and nurses. I saw them every day. Their kids were very adorable and always looked good and flashy. The teachers had distinctive uniforms that identified them, same as the nurses. Whenever I saw these teachers and nurses by the roadside waiting for taxis to go to school or the hospital, I admired them a lot. As young as I was, I had the desire to be like them. The way they used to dress, talk and even walk gave me a sense of inspiration.

Incidentally, I attended a girls' school which happened to be the demonstration school of a female college of education. For that reason, we had beautiful female teacher trainees trooping in our school yearly for their "out program". Their love and affection, warmth, beautiful words and actions really touched my heart. Their appearance, attitudes and words inspired me to want to be like them one day.

These formed part of the external motivation I had. Motivation is defined by a school of thought as a feeling of enthusiasm, interest or commitment that makes someone want to do something. It is the power that ignites you into doing what your heart desires.

Note that without commitment, there will be no results. If you are not internally motivated, you can't be committed. There is motivation behind every great success. I believe each and every one of us is good and can be better, everyone knows what is good and how to get it, but the question is; why aren't they doing it? There is something missing and that thing is motivation. There will be no achievement if you have nothing in your heart to give you the urge to move on. No one does something he hates and succeeds in it. Everyone who succeeds in his or her work loves what he or she does, hence the motivation to do more and come out the best.

Ideas are not adopted automatically; they are driven into practice with courageous patience.

Admiral Hyman Rickover.

Why do we need to be motivated?

A goal is like a brand new car that looks sparkling. Without a key you cannot start the car, it will remain dormant until you spark it with the key and accelerate. So our goals alone can't move us to the top. We need motivation as the key to drive them to materialize.

Also, with motivation, life becomes more meaningful and fulfilling. We all have the ability to achieve whatever goal we set for ourselves if only the goal is SMART; Specific, Measurable, Achievable, and Realistic and Time-bound. When you are internally motivated, you love whatever work you do. It makes you feel fulfilled and accomplished.

As human as we are, it is easy to give up when we encounter difficulties. Each and every one of us needs motivation to overcome challenges and win in life. Why would an athlete be in the track chasing the air in vain? There must be something a compelling prize; that is why that person runs to the end. The title or the fame, the certificate and medals are what motivate that athlete to run the race. We need to be motivated both internally and externally so as to be able to break through the hassles of life.

Believe in yourself. You are braver than you think, more talented than you can imagine.

Roy T. Bennett

How do I motivate myself?

Everything that we see outside of us is already inside of us. And all the answers to every question that we have in life, we have if we go deep within. The greatest journey you can ever take is a journey of self-discovery.

Ona Brown

If you want to make a way where there seems to be a roadblock, motivation is extremely essential. You must know how to motivate yourself. You should be able to keep your spirit high no matter how discouraging the

66

situation may be. That is the only way to get the power you need to overcome difficulties. You need to discover yourself; you need to know who you really are and what you want to be. Let's now look at the steps to follow in doing this.

1. Have a cause and stay focused.

To be able to build self-motivation, there are things which will be of great help to you as a youth. You should have *a cause*. A powerful source of motivation comes from having a cause you care about so much. My cause was walking out of poverty. Such cause can inspire you to give off your best even in the face of difficulties and can make you do the seemingly impossible things. I want to stress that, while other causes could inspire you temporarily, a cause that matters to you can inspire you forever. It becomes a fountain of motivation that will never dry.

As I indicated earlier, a dream is something you wish for strongly. Sometimes, your cause is a powerful source, yet it may be abstract in nature or intangible. That's why you have to make it realistic or concrete by writing it down.

For example, imagine how life would be if you got a good job to do. Imagine how good it would feel to be called a doctor, lawyer or anything you wish and the comfort that comes with it. It is important to have a dream because it's more difficult to get motivated if you have nothing as a target. I don't think you will be going to school if you have absolutely nothing in mind to become.

I want to add that, your dream must be big enough to inspire you. It must be something that can happen but challenges you. It must stretch your ability beyond your comfort zone.

Only as high as I reach can I grow, only as far as I seek can I go, only as deep as I look can I see, only as much as I dream can I be.

Karen Ravn

To be truly motivated, you must hunger for and not just desire. Having mere desire, won't take you through difficult times since you don't want it badly enough. In many cases, hunger makes the difference between best performers and the mediocre ones. To have hunger, your cause and your dream play a big role here. It makes you handle it like your very life depends on it and this pushes you automatically to work it out. If you have a cause you care so much about and a big dream related to it, you should have the hunger inside of you. When you feel you are losing your hunger, I encourage you to revisit your cause and the dream you have written down; that will ginger you to get back your hunger.

Wanting something is not enough. Your motivation must be absolutely compelling in order to overcome the obstacles that will invariably come your way.

68

Les Brown

Comparing yourself with others is an effective way of de-motivating yourself. Even if you start with enthusiasm, you will soon lose your energy when you compare yourself to others. Always know life is not a competition, we all have our own race to run so however others perform is irrelevant. Comparing yourself to others is like comparing the performance of a tortoise with a horse using the same standard. Bear in mind that the only competitor you have is your previous self.

When we meet obstacles on our way, the tendency to quit would be strong. Here, you feel it's too much to carry, too difficult to move on. You may feel that your dream is not realistic and thus cannot be achieved. That is a lie, that feeling is a distracter; something to veer you off your path to success. This is what makes someone a victor and the other a failure in the face of similar difficulties. In such cases, all you need to do is not to think about how to complete the race, but how to battle other possible setbacks awaiting you. Just focus on taking the next step.

Success is not final; failure is not fatal; it is the courage to continue that counts.

Winston Churchill

2. The use of positive affirmations

Another way to motivate yourself is by using affirmative words. The consistent use of affirmation is another way you can motivate yourself. Affirmation is the positive statement or declaration of the truth or existence of something. According to Jack Canfield and Mark Victor, authors of *Chicken Soup for the Soul,* a good affirmation has some key characteristics.

First of all, they suggested affirmations must start with "I am" they explained these are the two most powerful words in our daily vocabulary. Every word you say after these two words is taken directly by your system as an order. Even though you feel you are just describing a situation, it is taken by your subconscious mind as a command.

They added that affirmation must be stated in positive. One must avoid using negative words like "not". When you say "I am not afraid of this interview." Your system doesn't take the word "not" but takes "afraid." If I should tell you not to think of a lion, you would instantly think about it. The concept of lion overpowers the "not." They said that, it's better to tell your child "close the door softly" than to say, "don't slam the door". The child will not hear the "don't" but will just hear the "slam". This implies that when we use negative affirmations they have power over our positives. The subconscious mind is just like a child, so tell it what you want rather than what you don't want.

They also added that affirmations must be stated in present tense; say it as if it is happening now, that helps you to feel its existence. For example, "I am winning the prize".

Affirmations, they said, should be short and specific. An example is, "I am passing all six subjects with distinction. It should have verbs ending with -ing, and words that have feelings; e.g. "I am proudly receiving my Bachelor's degree at 22".

The final thing you should know is that affirmations are meant for yourself, not for someone else. All your affirmations should describe your own behavior and achievements not someone else's. Affirmations become motivation as you constantly and consistently use them daily. So avoid saying, "I will win like Kwame did".

3. Develop a positive self-image

How do you see yourself? What do you say you are? How do you portray yourself in the eyes of others? The image you have about yourself makes you either weak or strong. I have friends who say things like "I know I am not beautiful". Such a person has undermined herself therefore no matter how beautiful she dresses; all she sees in her mind is that she doesn't look good enough. If you see yourself that way, you have already lost yourself and have given other people power over you. Always see yourself among the best, think positively and think about all the good things inside of you.

How do others motivate us?

From the beginning, my parents had enough to cater for the small family they had. We were comfortable until the very day they lost everything and decided to leave me behind with my aunty to attend school as they go to till the land back at our village.

One thing I liked so much about them was their understanding of education. They valued education so much that they were prepared to do anything just to help us make it through. My father always said, "My father was a head teacher yet none of us his children was well-educated, but for you my children, I will till the ground until each of you gets a good education to enable you have a better life." Whenever he said this, with his kind of diction, I laughed; but today I got the real meaning of what he used to say.

I remember, I used to work with my mother to harvest cocoa. I would normally follow her with a basket running down the mountain diving and chasing escaping cocoa pod down the hill. She would ferment, dry the seeds and sell them in order to pay our fees. She was a hardworking woman who did her best to ensure that she had enough money to pay our fees and feed us while my father went back to school.

I remember my mother would send words to me to wait for her by the road side so she could get me some salted fish, gari, cassava dough, beans, dry maize and some vegetables on her return from a popular market (Abotoase). She always advised me to be serious with my books and make her proud. She denied buying herself good clothes and always wore her old dresses just to save money for our education.

This is what I call external motivation. My parents did their part motivating me in diverse ways. I remember when I told my dad about the access course, he was so happy and said he would do anything just to get me there. When I called him that I wasn't picked, he asked me to do a follow-up, because it may be a mistake. When I told him on the second time that I was sacked and he said to me, "May be this is not your time, God knows best, keep praying and God is in control."

If you are a parent or a guardian reading this, I have a question for you. How do you motivate your children? My aunty was my inspiration; she encouraged me to take the exams again which made my grades one step better. Her words and sometimes gifts as reward for achievements were motivating factors. My parent's suffering, which I witnessed and experienced was another source of motivation. These experiences kept me going; they molded me into a responsible and hardworking woman. It also urged me on to keep fighting and boosted my tenacity and confidence.

Everyone needs motivation to ginger the desire for greatness and look beyond the failures of life.

One day, I had a conversation with one of my mentees about life and motivation. He shared a touching story of his life and I want to share with you. He narrated that when he completed senior high school, he went to work in order to earn some money to further his education.

In the process of working, he got so much money and misused it because he didn't know what it meant to save or invest. Because he made an appreciable stash of cash, he decided he was content in life and did not find the need to go to school anymore. He continued that way for three years before one day he travelled home. There he saw his juniors and other colleagues whom they used to tease in class now in tertiary institutions and others already professionals. According to him, that made him feel as if he had wasted his time. When he cast his mind back to assess what he had done, he realized he had wasted the money he made over the period, as he couldn't account for it.

74

I want to say that money has power to make and unmake you. If you get it too early, with inexperience, it could be a problem. It can make you proud, complacent and careless, leading to your destruction. He came to a decision there and then; he made up his mind to set his mother up with a business with the little money left and go back to school.

Merely watching others progress motivated him to make a better decision. As I write, he is a professional teacher and has taught for over 6 years now. Let's learn from people's mistakes as youth. There are a lot of motivational speakers who put their life experiences in books for us to buy and use to help ourselves. The issue now is how many of us would buy a book just to get motivated? We would rather dress well than get our library stuffed with books that will build, energize and inspire us to achieve excellence in life.

There is this adage, "When you don't want it to get burnt, it would never get cooked". You need to make a lot of sacrifices in life in order to get doors to open for you. You can be young or old; but only sacrifice can lead to many achievements.

I have benefitted greatly from sacrifice. We all know the saying, "There are more blessings in giving than in receiving". The question now is; how many of us prefer to give than to receive? Often times, people expect immediate compensation for all they do, but with a little sacrifice they could have achieved much more later on.

75

It's time to learn to sacrifice our time, money and energy for others so as to establish rapport that will make way for us in the near future. In sacrifice, we don't look forward for immediate reward; it will come by itself in due course. Sacrifice helps our work to go forward but many people don't know. Allow yourself to be motivated by others; let their words, actions and in actions propel you into success.

Someone needs your actions to inspire his actions. Never forget, your little broken cake is someone's daily meal! Care to share your little cake!

Israelmore Ayivor

Be your own inspiration

I completed High School and had no money to continue. I had passion for construction so I went to the village where I hail from to help my family. I helped my grandmother in selling gari and corn dough; I had to carry this from house to house to sell.

I then moved to my maternal uncle at Vakpo and started a garden egg farm. The farm was very far so we had to walk nearly two hours to and from the farm. In the evenings, I sold hot beverages (tea, hot chocolate with its accompaniments such as toast and omelet) to make extra income; I did that for three years.

I got a carpenter to make me a wooden moneybox and started savings. Later, I traveled to Accra to work with a big construction

76

firm where I was paid daily for carrying mortar. I saved my wages and also got the opportunity to network with some great personalities. I was able to use my strength and the natural resource I had to gather the funds I needed to be able to enroll in the polytechnic where I read construction technician courses 1, 2 and 3.

During this time, I continued to work with some construction companies. I was also providing barbering services for my mates from dormitory to dormitory.

During the mandatory post-tertiary national service period, I read about a program dubbed 'Leaders Factory' in the newspapers. I attended the program, where I bought a little book titles "Wellspring of Wisdom" by Gideon Titi-Ofei. In the book, I read a statement that said, "Life is full of a lot of closed doors and wisdom is the ability to identify the right key in the right door".

Further the author explained that no amount of prayer can spark a car; what you need is to identify the right key, turn on the ignition, spark the car, change the gear and start moving. That was the turning point in my life. It opened my eyes to the fact that I am responsible for turning my life around. Like a car, I needed to be my own motivation.

I had to do all it takes to become a better person and have a better life. This inspired me to pursue a degree in quantity surveying and construction economics. Subsequently, I started my own construction firm.

Pastor Hayford A. Honitse

That is the story of my friend, Pastor Hayford; he went through similar things as I did. I was a maidservant, I had to do a lot of hard labor and render services to get paid. As mentioned earlier, in college I had to start photography on commercial basis without a camera to raise funds to support my family. I was once a hawker; I sold different things at the Hohoe lorry park. At night, I sold fruits by the roadside. I did all these in my bid to raise funds for my sisters and me.

As you work tirelessly to pave a way through the hassles, never forget that money is not everything. Hold yourself accountable and keep your integrity intact by engaging only in legitimate and ethical endeavors to make money. When you are internally motivated, you are able to do any good to help you accomplish your aims

I was motivated.

I completed junior high school and for almost twenty years, I didn't even go for my result slip; I have been married for ten years. One day I went to church and after closing I decided to walk with a sister home. Out of our conversation she got to know I had completed junior high school and asked why I didn't continue my education in spite of the fact that I was fluent in English. She asked about my results. When I told her that I had aggregate 20, she seemed happy, knowing that I schooled in the village. She wondered if I would love to return to school if someone is willing to help out. I enthusiastically responded in the affirmative.

She encouraged me to think about it seriously. I made up my mind instantly. I mustered courage and informed my husband that I wanted to go back to school. After 10 years of marriage, telling him this was shocking but he was more than happy to support me.

I am now in the third year of senior high school and performing marvelously to my surprise with the final exam right ahead of me. It's my dream to be a lecturer and if not for the words of motivation I heard from a friend, this dream would have died. They were just a few words of motivation she gave me and I am now on the way to be a career woman.

I am no more a woman who sells spices and vegetables on a tray for survival. I can now be a woman who support her husband and not depend on him for virtually every need. I have been motivated by my friend, my mum, my husband and above all my personal motivation.

Stella

The power of perspiration
The heights that great men reached and kept were not attained by sudden flight: but they, whilst their companions slept, were burning the midnight candle.

Heny Wadsworth Longfellow

To be able to pave way through the hassles of life, you need to be ready to perspire. Many people want to attain higher heights, yet they are not ready to get on the ground, sweat and get dirty. So long as the level of excellence you crave for is not yet at hand, you have to keep perspiring till you grab it. Even then, you need to work harder to sustain it; else you can easily lose it in a twinkle of an eye.

The outcome of perspiration is the realization of your dreams and desires. Your good thoughts and ideas will remain a desire if you refuse to get to work and sweat them into fruition. Our ability to solve the problems we encounter gives us the strength and knowledge we need to survive the battles ahead.

After I was granted the opportunity to join the access course, I kept the phrase, "You have to prove yourself" in mind every day and took it as a challenge. Due to that, when I joined my colleagues at the center for the course, I had to put in more efforts than everyone else. This was because classes had started three weeks before I got there. With this in mind, I approached my mates, collected and copied all the notes they were given prior to my arrival and asked someone to explain them to me. I realized that if I wanted to make my dreams, desires, and aspirations come alive, I had to work extra hard for it. I was ready to sacrifice my sleep to pay the price for my dream.

I put in lots of effort, I strived harder but if it were my effort alone I might still be hassling by now. That critical moment, God did a miracle; he realized my efforts from the very beginning and gave me what I asked of him. Believe in yourself, what you are doing and above all, believe in God. I believed in no one else but me, I saw the course as an opportunity to seize and God took care of the rest.

In my class at the time, there were different kinds of students. Those who came to display luxury, compete in fashion, enlarge their scope of friends, and those who came just to have a feel of the course. The ones like me, who had no other options, were there for one reason; to make it through to college by all means. I was the quiet type in class and hardly answered questions. It was a battle of survival of the fittest and one needed to have the determination and perseverance to be able to sail through.

I knew I was a slow learner; therefore, I paid for extra tuition. I had registered to rewrite the private exam so I took the chance to attend extra classes in mathematics with great seriousness together with what we were being taught at the access course centre.

In addition to these, I drew a timetable for studies after identifying my best study time to be at dawn. I placed all the challenging topics on the time table for dawn studies. I spent shorter hours at preps and slept early. This allowed me to wake up around 4am while others were snoring. Surprisingly, although we were all there to study for a chance to obtain higher education, the night was all about talking for many students. Preps turned into chitchat time. In the midst of all these ups and downs, I had the first position in our mock exams in a class of over 30 students with 84%. At the end of the course we all went back to our various homes waiting for our results and postings.

One evening, Ankey a friend of mine came over to my house and broke the news that the results were out. We took out half-dead torchlight and started our journey to the school premises that night. Anxiety could not allow me to sleep without knowing whether or not I had gotten a school. When we got there, I was mesmerized to see my name on the second list of names. I could not understand how my name would be on the second list out of about 1000 names. Amazingly, I was given my first choice school; St Francis College of Education. I could not believe my eyes. I was shocked to my bones that I made it after being called a failure. That was how I went to the teacher training college. I was really happy and realized it pays to be hard working, focused and perspire.

Start by doing what is necessary for your achievement; then do what's possible; and suddenly you are doing the impossible to get you to your dreams.

Francis of Assisi

Use your compass to your advantage

I once watched a video clip titled, "The compass." It started by asking questions that required critical thinking such as, "What will you do right now if you knew you could use your compass to get past any failure?" It explained "the compass" as one's inner sense of direction, the road that guides you to the fulfillment of your greatest dream. Your compass, according to the clip, is what enables you to tap into the inner part of you which knows how to do more, be more and give more to the world. Also, your compass is your inner voice and vision, intuition and inspiration that are guiding, prompting and refining you to your magnificence.

Now imagine that you wake up one day and just find yourself on a desert, what will come into your mind first? Perhaps, it will be fear of going further; fear of going left, right, back or front. I encourage you to see each day of your life as a desert without any hope and think of how to create life on that desert to sustain you. You don't have to wait there for the right time to know more and do more; you are already on your journey of life so live it. You are already on this journey – a world filled with uncertainties, hardship, despair and negativity. The time to decide what becomes of you on that desert is now.

On that desert, you are lost, you are lonely, and have gotten to a point where you stand alone. That should not change the course of your life and aspirations but rather energize you to take a step further. This is how life is; you need to gather courage because you have no one else but you. You need to cultivate in you, a sense of self-love.

Most successful people whom we hear about today had difficult patches too. Do you know why they stand out? Because they rather turned these challenges into opportunities hence creating the desired reality they have today which you wish to be a part of. Your future is in your hands; your first step can lead you to an amazing place if you have the inner will to carry on.

You have to get things going now; there is no perfect timing, the time to make a difference is in your youth. You need to take an inspired action, pay attention to yourself and follow your inner guidance. You can't be what you don't want to be; you can't build anything without a strong foundation. Even in our villages where people use mud to build houses, they still have a way of laying a firm foundation with stones. You need to establish your foundation; this foundation is based on your self-esteem; what you think to be true about yourself and your confidence. Your core values are very essential; know who you are where you are coming from and where you want to be.

Success is an endless journey without a destination; you must keep winning till your last breath fades away.

My career as a teacher

I was posted to a deprived school where the classrooms were dilapidated and classes were combined due to inadequate number of teachers. That echoed how I suffered growing up; I felt the pain of these innocent children who sometimes came to school on empty stomach and others had neither exercise books nor slippers on their feet. I was drawn to their difficulties, got energized to help give them a future and vowed to make a change in their lives.

Meeting a school where the children could neither read with understanding nor write simple essays, I adopted a technique using story pictures and word association to assist them to write short stories. Amazingly, within three to four years, these same children sat for BECE and had 100%. In 2015, this method won me the Bayport Teacher Innovation Award as an innovative way of teaching reading and writing. I have since replicated this project in in over 500 schools training over 1700 teachers in 10 districts of the Volta Region.

One thing I also did was to start looking out for support to change the conditions of the classrooms. I was lucky to have found a non-profit called Adanu to build a three-unit classroom block for our kindergarten which was then housed in "a blue kiosk." Soon, my head teacher also got Pencils of Promise to build another three units of the six-unit classroom blocks they promised to provide my school.

Today, with a team of committed and hardworking teachers and a visionary head teacher, a school which for over 20 years could not boast of JHS graduates, the school has many students graduating from SHS with some going to various tertiary institutions with the hope of furthering their education and contributing to the development of their community.

If a person who was called a failure could rise to this level and keep climbing, then what excuse do you have to fail at life? Where ever you find yourself, no matter how messed up the environment may be, find a good reason to be happy and make it home. Endeavour to be the reason why there comes a change and development. Be the reason why someone goes a step higher and draws a step closer to his or her dreams.

Giving back

Growing up, my dream was to be a renowned journalist, but I couldn't reach that dream due to financials challenges. After grabbing a career in teaching, I launched into the same job using my God-given talent. I designed a radio talk show Cohesive Youth Platform (CYPLAT), focused on discussing issues affecting the youth; education, career development and women empowerment. Soon the then general manger saw my passion and added two more of the stations shows for me to host. I joyfully hosted Health is Wealth, Best Wishes and CYPLAT shows for six years. I also helped design a children's program hosted by children we groomed. All these were done voluntarily without salaries just passion and satisfaction from the lives

86

that are impacted. At a point when the station needed money to run, I raised funds and started paying for the airtime for CYPLAT show to be sustained on air.

This has been my way of giving back to society; it is a satisfying and fulfilling hobby, which made me come alive. I made a lot of friends and gave hope to thousands of listeners. As I touch lives through these programs, I was receiving my share of wisdom, blessings and refining my skills and resume.

My passion for women and girls' empowerment led to the establishment of my NGO; Feminine Star Africa. I have trained and employed a team of young women working vigorously to give other women the voice they need and the platform to realise their fullest potentials. When I see the capabilities of women while some live as though they were slaves, others as if they have no choices, it breaks my heart.

Every woman should know and tap into her strength for greatness. We are grooming both boys and girls through our seminars to understand themselves, build self-esteem and confidence. We share our experiences to inspire them to believe they too can be anything they dream of. We are giving off ourselves to help them become resourceful citizens. I believe we can eliminate poverty if we teach young men and women to identify and nurture their potentials to the fullest.

When God rewards your hassles

To crown it all, in 2017, I was selected to participate in the Mandela Washington Fellowship for young African leaders in the United States of America. It was a six-week program designed by the US government to identify young leaders making impact in their communities. The selection process was very competitive; over 4,600 young people applied in Ghana and only 40 were of us selected. There were over 60,000 applications from the whole Continent and only 1,000 were selected. Being a part of the 40 people from Ghana and part of the 10% of the 1000 chosen to do a further six-week internship was a great inspiration to me.

Aside the skills and network acquired, my short stay in the US has cleared a lot of misconceptions I had. I have learned that everybody has great potential but there is the need for preparation before any opportunity will be beneficial. Just like Ghana, there are so many poor people in the US; there are homeless people living their lives on the streets, including children. This got me wondering, if Americans could lose all they have and end up on the streets, what happens to people who migrate illegally? How could they survive in a country where if you have no money, you have no food coupled with a terrible weather; winter which could get so cold?

With this enlightenment, I so much appreciate how blessed we are to have such priceless resources as a country. I however do feel very ashamed and very disappointed that we are unable to manage these resources to benefit all Ghanaians. I do sincerely believe that when we break the chain of corruption, individualism and think nationally, it will liberate our country and the African Continent as a whole. We must rise to our fullest glory and the change starts with YOU!

With all the above accomplishments chopped, I wake up daily feeling I have the ability to do better and I take responsibility for the things that aren't going well. If I still have this feeling of dissatisfaction, then what are you doing sitting down expecting manner to fall? This simply explains that, success is never enough; you have to keep working hard and smart every day because many lives depend on your success to succeed. Remember what I said earlier that, "Success is an endless journey without a destination; you must keep winning till your last breath fades away."

Be determined to change your situation; be determined to raise your life from the base to the apex. Life is about challenging your present self, not challenging others. The choice is in your hands and you have all it takes to be great; start living your greatness now!

Disability is not inability

I became paraplegic at the age of 7, as a result of a medical error. Despite all obstacles, I continued my primary and secondary education and passed all my examinations. I have been working for 18 years now, driving my own car everyday independently. Looking at the benefits of being independent, I decided to venture into freelance graphic design and computer maintenance; then later joined a call centre business. My success at the call centre informed my promotion to supervisory and managerial roles within 3 years. I then moved on to an international bank where I worked for 7 years as Trade Finance Assistant; a position I resigned from to devote my time to volunteering with various non-profits.

I started with the non-profit organization called Fraternité Mauricienne des Malades et Handicapés (FMMH). FMMH is a sport club where I functioned as a wheelchair basketball player, accountant and HR administrator. As a passionate wheelchair basketball player, I worked as assistant coach for the FMMH sports club. I found myself getting more satisfaction from the work, even when it was unpaid, than all the previous years I had spent working for huge amounts of money. My work is about helping young boys and girls with different disabilities to succeed and this brings me so much more joy.

In 2017, I was awarded a scholarship under the Mandela Washington Fellowship program to study and do an internship in the United States of America for three months. After the Fellowship I joined the Non-profit called Dis-Moi (Droits Humains Ocean Indien) where I am currently working as program manager and leader of the Commission for the Rights of People with Disabilities.

After winning several honours in wheelchair basketball in Mauritius, I moved to Sheffield in the United Kingdom in 2012 to train and play with the Sheffield Stealers for a month. During the Mandela Washington Fellowship program, I had the chance to play in the Summer League with the Phoenix Wheelchair Suns. After each of these experiences, I applied what I had learned as player and coach to the wheelchair basketball team to help the youth in the team develop to become better players.

My vision is to help as many disabled persons as possible have access to proper education, work, sports and leisure by encouraging them to develop their potential. I fight for the well-being of children and adults with multiple disabilities. I do this by soliciting for and making appropriate use of aids through collaboration with government agencies and private firms. This helps them to participate in the community life of Mauritius, making them independent enough to be able to participate in all activities not merely as beneficiaries but also as potential and actual providers.

I believe that the opportunity to participate in the political, economic and social life of our own community is a basic right. I believe that public buildings should be accessible to all citizens with disabilities. I also believe that all citizens with disabilities should be afforded space in the workplace to give them the opportunity of employment within their abilities - not their disabilities. Disability is part of the human experience and it in no way diminishes the right of individuals to live independently.

I am committed to ensuring that all people with disabilities have a right to equal opportunity, to be economically self-sufficient, and to earn and save without jeopardizing access to the services and support systems that allow them to live and work independently.

Jean Francois Favory,
Wheelchair Basketball Player/ Mandela Washington Fellow 2017/
Program Manager and Leader of the Commission for the Rights of
People with Disabilities at Dis-Moi
(MAURITIUS)

Wiyaala – The Lioness of Africa

I was faced with many hurdles as a child. Some of them were as a result of my father being married to three women and having many children. We being girls, we were not valued and hence no seriousness was attached to our education. My family faced many financial challenges and even shelter on our heads was at times very challenging. I was shut down by many relatives including my parents and was told, "Children don't speak when adults speak". This led me to develop resistance which made many people in my family call me names. Some even thought I was a witch as they were thinking only a witch could be that resistant to the authority of adults.

As a teenager, I started facing the issues of bullying as many people were thinking I was not feminine enough. There were countless occasions where my mother was asked if I was a girl or a boy. Most people didn't accept me as I was and I couldn't make friends as well because I was always the odd one out.

Regardless of all these challenges I was persistent and determined to have a better life. I did well through junior and senior high school and got admitted into a Polytechnic. Sadly, I had to drop out of school after the first few semesters due to financial challenges; I couldn't pay my fees. With these challenges hindering my education, I decided to explore my talents to make a career out of it. I decided to step out and do what I love which is dancing and singing. I performed at various shows in my small community of Tumu in the Upper West Region of Ghana.

93

My first performance was a dance competition. When I registered I didn't have any costume to wear. I had to borrow my elder sister's oversized snickers. I made my own dress from pieces of cloth and made a belt out of my mother's tablecloth. Amazingly, I came out as the best dancer and winner of that competition.

With regular and frequent performances, I began to attract people and friends. One day a group of friends recommended that I try Stars Of The Future, which was a music reality TV show. I watched the show and instantly developed a strong desire to participate in it. I remembered how I used to stand in front of the mirror pretending I was receiving an award as a musician. With my little savings at hand, I set off to Accra with optimism to audition and win the show.

In spite of all my practice and preparation, I auditioned and was given a BIG NO! I was so hurt but not discouraged. I chose to try the second time and it was still a NO! With a relentless spirit, I tried the third time at Stars of the Future and this time around, it was a Yes! I was super excited and couldn't wait to take the stage; except that the Show was abruptly called off. Wow! At this point, I began to wonder if I was cursed.

Then I heard about Vodafone Icons, another music TV reality show. I went there as well with the hope of making it through. Unfortunately, I was still given a big fat NO! Luckily, Stars of the Future sorted out their issues and called us to return to the competition in 2011. I was in at last! That was where my breakthrough began. I managed to make it through to second runner-up. In 2012, I prepared well and after a series of training and performance sessions, I won at Vodafone Icons and got two cars and a recording contract as a prize!

I now have many songs and a very good manager who has been very supportive of my career and is always pushing for my success. I have travelled around the world performing on great platforms I never imagined. I have won several awards including African Music Award, Ghana Music Award Song Writer of the Year, Best Vocalist of the Year and Glitz Style Award – Best Individual Style Awards. My region has recognised my efforts by awarding me with the Youth Achievers Award as the Music Ambassador. My community has also awarded me with Sisala Prestigious Award and had named a street after me.

I am sharing my story in Rita's book You Are Unstoppable! Reach Your Goals In Spite Of Obstacles because, I am the epitome of this statement. I rose from nothing except a dream and inspiration from listening and watching Madonna on a video in the village to become the Lioness of Africa.

This is just my beginning, I will keep going higher until I am no more and even that, my legacy will live on. After all the above accomplishments, I still feel a boundless energy and a strong belief that there is so much more to accomplish.

If, from nothing, I am here today, then what excuse do you have for giving up after just one try? This was possible because I believed in myself, my talent and didn't allow anyone to limit me. My advice to you is, you are the only one who knows what you have inside of you; your talent and abilities. All you need to do is make a move – don't sit and watch things happen. Even if you are from a rich home, take a step into greatness with optimism. You have to stand and fight for yourself. And when you go wrong, accept your mistakes learn from them, seek knowledge and soar higher.

Don't allow people to intimidate you; don't let the NO bring down your spirit, always rise above people's thoughts about you. Believing in yourself works the magic; don't look too far for what you want. Look inside you any time you are faced with hardships or challenges. You have all it takes to birth the star inside of you, believe YOU ARE UNDSTOPPABLE AND REACH YOUR GOALS IN SPITE OF ALL THE CHALLENGES.

Noella Wiyaala Nwadei,
Award - Winning Musician and band member, GRRRL
(GHANA)

PROFILE OF RITA SIAW

Rita Siaw started life from a very humble beginning living with her aunt. She went through a lot of struggles to complete her junior and senior high education. She trained as a professional teacher and taught for 9 years in a deprived government school where she played the roles of Assistant Head Teacher, Curriculum Leader as well as Guidance and Counseling Coordinator. She won Most Innovative Teacher Award in 2015/2016 and has replicated her innovations in other schools through Teacher Capacity Building Workshops on Pragmatic Reading and Writing as well as Positive Discipline in place of Corporal Punishment.

With her passion for journalism, she designed and hosted three radio shows to educate the public on health, youth and women-related issues voluntarily for six years. Rita Siaw founded Feminine Star Africa, a non-profit with the aim of improving rural education and advocating for the rights and empowerment of women and children. She is an inspirational speaker who shares her life to inspire students to change their mindset, set goals and build confidence.

She supports the reentry of teen mothers to school and gives skills training to unemployed women. Rita holds a Bachelor's degree in Education from University of Education, Winneba, Ghana. She is currently the Associate Director of Adanu, a non-profit focused on providing educational infrastructure. She is a 2017 Mandela Washington Fellow.